IMAGES
of America

PITMAN

A PITMAN CAMP MEETING TENT, C. 1875. This picture shows two unidentified women in front of their tent in Pitman Grove. Pitman Grove was a Methodist religious camp meeting place where tents were used as residences during the summer. This changed in the late 1880s, when cottages began to be built for the summer visitors.

IMAGES
of America

PITMAN

Michael D. Batten Jr. and Ralph J. Richards Jr.

ARCADIA
PUBLISHING

Published by Arcadia Publishing
Charleston, South Carolina

Library of Congress Catalog Card Number: 2002103051

For all general information contact Arcadia Publishing at:
Telephone 843-853-2070
Fax 843-853-0044
E-mail sales@arcadiapublishing.com
For customer service and orders:
Toll-Free 1-888-313-2665

Visit us on the Internet at www.arcadiapublishing.com

PITMAN GROVE PHOTOGRAPHER
J.H. ELTON, c. 1905. J.H. Elton was a
renowned photographer in the early 1900s.
She took most of the photographs used for
postcards in Pitman Grove and surrounding
areas. This real photo postcard shows Elton
in her studio.

CONTENTS

An Aerial View of Pitman Grove, c. 1960. The Pitman Grove Camp Meeting Auditorium is in the center of Pitman Grove. To the lower left is the McBurney ball field. To the lower right are Shertel Park and the tennis courts.

INTRODUCTION

In June 1871, the town of Pitman Grove was born from Methodist camp meeting roots. A group of ministers was searching for a "convenient and desirable" setting, and the 70 acres of oak and chestnut trees were the perfect spot to build their summer resort. The Pitman Grove Camp Meeting Auditorium was built in the center, with 12 avenues radiating out like the spokes of a wheel. A circular street extended around the outer rim of this wheel.

The first camp meeting was started in August 1871. Some 600 tents lined the avenues. By 1873, the first houses were beginning to replace the tents. By the early 1880s, the tents disappeared to give way to gravel walks, a store, a barbershop, restaurants, a butcher shop, and nearly 300 small cottages. These cottages were unique with their distinctive latticework and second floors that overhung the front porches. By 1900, a town with a permanent population had sprung up beyond the Pitman Grove area.

This book contains some wonderful photographs of a bygone era and features such places as Alcyon Park, the Pitman Camp Meeting, and Alcyon Track. Alcyon Park ran from the 1890s to World War II. After 130 years, the Pitman Camp Meeting Association still meets on Sunday evenings in the summer. Alcyon Track was one of the premier tracks of its day. Over the years, it raced bicycles, horses, and cars.

ACKNOWLEDGMENTS

When you take the time and effort to amass a collection of memorabilia, sharing it with others makes it all worthwhile. We would like to thank the following people for their generosity in sharing their photographs and memories.

Walter Chernokal, Bob Sweeten, Herb Vail, Phil Harms, Frank Smith, Bruce Craig, Russ Dodge, and John Collier provided many of the photographs for the Alcyon Track chapters. Richard Mangano supplied numerous photographs from the 1940s and 1950s. The Highland Chemical Engine Company, Pitman Fire Patrol, and Pitman Fire Company No. 1 loaned photographs from their private collections for use in this book. Thanks also go to the First Baptist Church of Pitman and the Church of the Good Shepherd for their help.

Two out-of-print books were very helpful: the Maple Press Company's *A History of Pitman, New Jersey* (1955), by Dr. Harold F. Wilson, and Taylor Publishing Company's *Pitman: A Town for All Seasons* (1979), by the Heritage of Pitman Book Committee.

Mike Batten Jr. would like to thank his wife, Bobbie, who makes anything and everything possible. Ralph Richards Jr. would like to thank his wife, Marcia, for typing, proofreading, and organizing this book. We could not have done this book without her.

One

PITMAN GROVE

THE PITMAN GROVE CAMP MEETING AUDITORIUM, C. THE 1940S. This building was used for summer religious camp meeting services held by different traveling ministers. Note the gingerbread on the houses along First Avenue.

A FAMILY PHOTOGRAPH, 1905. Note the coats and hats on the children. The message on the postcard reads, "We just run in to wish you all a Merry Xmas & Happy New Year."

A FAMILY ON ONE OF THE AVENUES, 1905. The members of this family have their flags up for the Fourth of July celebration.

HOUSES ON WEST AVENUE. The house to the left has a tower room and notable gingerbread. The house to the right was known as the Bethel House.

SHREVE COTTAGE, WEST AVENUE, 1915. This is a real photo postcard to a Germantown neighbor. The message reads, "This is our cottage, we like it here very much. Would like very much to have you and Mary come down and spend the day some Saturday or Sunday before we come home. Phone to Harry."

11

THE BITTING FAMILY, 1901. The location shown in this photograph is believed to be Southwest Avenue. Supposedly, the picture was taken by W.C.K. Walls. Note the woman with the photograph album.

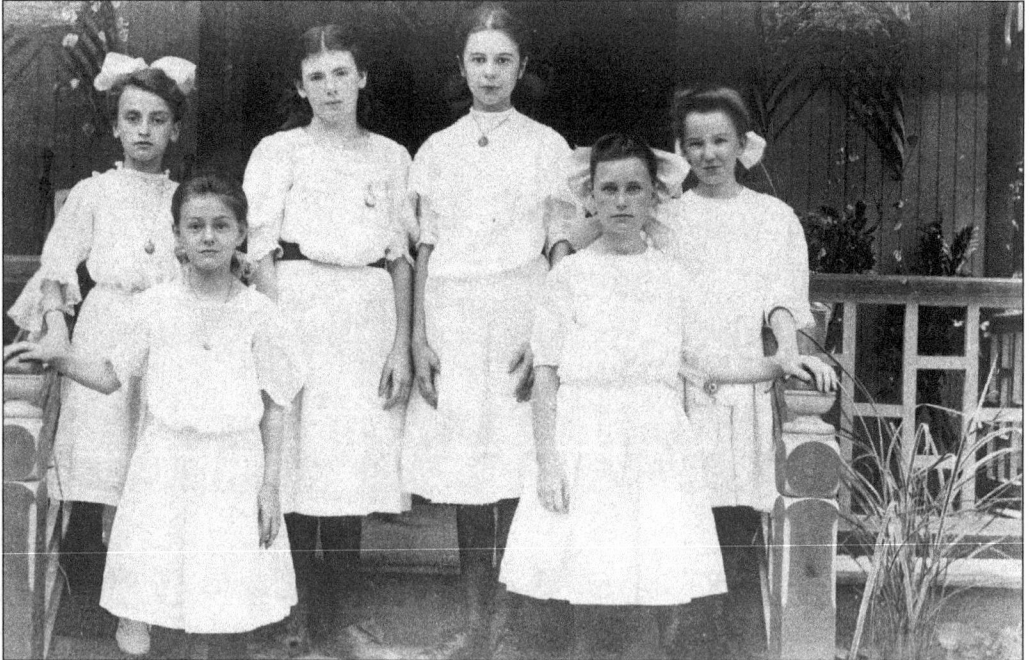

MEMBERS OF THE SIGMA CAPPA CLUB, 1906. These women were members of some sort of sorority of the day. The postcard was mailed in September 1906 to Hannah McCarson from Salem.

THE PITMAN FIRE COMPANY WAGON, 1907. Young ladies are shown with the latest fire equipment. The Pitman Fire Company wagon is loaded with fire extinguishers.

THE PITMAN CONCERT BAND, 1910. This band started in late November 1910. It consisted of 28 instruments and was under the leadership of Frank Lanning. It debuted in the Glassboro Thanksgiving Day Parade. More than 200 Pitmanites bought train tickets to see the band perform that day.

A TENTH AVENUE RESTAURANT, PITMAN GROVE, 1905. With the influx of so many people into Pitman Grove, restaurants, barbershops, and rooming houses popped up everywhere. Note the Focer and Paulin horse and wagon.

THE W.C.K. WALLS HOUSE. The Fourth of July in Pitman was a special time, as exemplified by W.C.K. Walls's house. A writer for the *Pitman Grove Review*, W.C.K. Walls was also a fireman and head of the committee for the granite boulder commemorating Pitman men who served in World War I. A school on Grant Avenue bears his name.

14

THE LIZZIE SMITH TEMPLE. The Lizzie Smith Temple was built in 1896 and named for Lizzie Smith, who was a successful evangelist of her time. The temple was erected on the corner of South and Wesley Avenues in Pitman Grove and seated 700 people. The first service was on Friday, July 31, 1896. The sign on the tree is an advertisement for the *Philadelphia Public Ledger*.

THE DEMOLITION OF THE LIZZIE SMITH TEMPLE, SEPTEMBER 1958. After 62 years, the Lizzie Smith Temple was torn down.

THE PITMAN GROVE ARCH, 1909. This arch was the entrance to Pitman Grove in the late 19th century. The sign to the right reads, "Bicycles must not enter gate." The gate was located at First Avenue and Broadway. The Pitman Rotary Club placed a new one there in 1970.

34th Annual Report

OF THE

PITMAN

COTTAGERS' ASSOCIATION

(Incorporated)

PITMAN, NEW JERSEY

SEASON OF 1933

Officers and Committees for 1934

NOTICES

Regular Meetings—First Monday evening in April, June, July, August and first Tuesday after first Monday in September.

Annual Meeting—For election of officers, etc., third Monday evening in August.

Ladies' Auxiliary—Meets the second and fourth Monday evenings in June, July, August and the second Monday evening in September.

OFFICERS FOR 1934

President	MATTHEW KENNEY
Vice-President	HARRY BARNETT
Treasurer	CHARLES W. LAMBERT
Secretary	RUSSELL E. SWALM

TRUSTEES

Robert Withington	Term Expires	1934
Frank M. Dealy	" "	
Mahlon Saunders	" "	
Philip S. Francis	" "	1935
Samuel T. Hudson	" "	
Harry L. Chrisman	" "	
Harry Churen	" "	1936
Harry Hewett	" "	
John D. Beck	" "	

AN ANNUAL REPORT OF THE PITMAN COTTAGERS' ASSOCIATION, 1933. This report lists all 342 members' names and addresses. The officers and committees for the 1934 season are also included. The treasurer's report shows a spending of $4,313.23 during the year.

A PITMAN GROVE HOUSE, 1906. This is a typical Pitman Grove house of the early 20th century. The front room upstairs hangs over the front porch. The house has a seamed metal roof and fish scales above the upstairs windows. It also has double-wide front doors.

CAMP MEETING DAY, 1905. This view offers a good idea of just how many people lived in Pitman Grove at the time.

CONTRACTORS WORK TO SAVE THE PITMAN GROVE CAMP MEETING AUDITORIUM, 1960. The auditorium, in the center of Pitman Grove, was built in the early 1870s. It still stands today after a complete restoration in the 1990s.

FIRST AVENUE, PITMAN GROVE, C. 1950. To the right is a taxi stand and Chris' Quaker Store. This store sold meats, groceries, and frozen foods. Notice the houses as they stood some 70 years after they were built.

FOURTH AVENUE, LOOKING NORTH TO HOLLY AVENUE, 1907. Note the gate at the end of Fourth Avenue. This was another entrance into Pitman Grove. The house on Holly Avenue still stands today.

THE BUILDING LOTS KNOWN AS THE PITMAN HIGHLANDS, 1907. The Pitman Highlands, or Pancoast Tract, were between North Broadway and the railroad. This area included land around Colonial Avenue. The lots were 60 by 150 feet and sold for about $150 apiece.

A Pitman Grove Cottage, 1910. The cottage Tioga was typical of the gingerbread houses that replaced the tents that started the Pitman Grove area. This cottage was located on the corner of Third and East Avenues.

A Pitman Schoolhouse, 1905. Built in July 1884, this schoolhouse was located at the corner of Summit and Holly Avenues. Edwin Oshandis is in the front to the right.

PITMAN GROVE PUBLIC SCHOOL.

Report of *Eva M. Cheesman*

For month ending *Dec. 25* 189 *6.*

Reading,	*98*	Physiology,	*95*
Orthography,	*97*	Composition,	
Arithmetic,	*95*	Drawing,	
Geography,	*85*	Book-keeping,	
Penmanship,	*90*		
Grammar, *Language*	*93*		
Etymology,		Deportment, *100*	
History,	*91*	General average, *93*	
Algebra,		No. of days present,	*18*
Philosophy,		No. of days absent,	*2*
Civil Government,		No. of times tardy,	*8*

Average time per day spent in study at home, *50 minutes.*

Explanation:—100 is the Maximum; 90 to 100, Excellent; 80 to 90 Good; 70 to 80, Fair. Below 70 is unsatisfactory.

Remarks:

Pitman Grove, N. J., *Jan. 1* 189 *7*

EMMA E. RULON, Teacher.

A PITMAN GROVE PUBLIC SCHOOL REPORT CARD, JANUARY 1, 1897. Eva M. Cheesman's report card shows that her teacher was Emma E. Rulon. It also shows that there were permanent residents in the Pitman Grove area in the late 1890s even though Pitman was known as a summer resort at that time.

A COTTAGE IN THE PITMAN GROVE AREA, 1999. This cottage, located at 192 North Avenue, combines 19th-century charm with 20th-century needs.

THE SUMMIT PARK PAVILION, THE "SHELL," 1905. The Shell was erected in 1898 and was enlarged in 1900 by the Pitman Cottagers' Association. It was attached to the rear of the Pitman Fire Patrol building.

PITMAN GROVE HOUSES, THE 1940s. This view offers an example of just how close many of the cottages were. The porch roofs almost seem to touch.

Two

ALCYON TRACK

A WATER WAGON AT ALCYON TRACK, 1927. Halsey Cheesman is sitting on the water wagon after watering the track for the day's events. Harness racing was in its heyday in the 1920s and 1930s.

HARNESS RACING AT ALCYON TRACK, C. 1927. Horse and driver are shown posing on the track. This picture also shows an advertisement for Alcyon Park, painted on the roof of one of the stables in the background.

RED MAN'S DAY AT ALCYON PARK, 1916. This photograph shows the beginning of a match race between a Mr. Green of Salem in a Ford and a Mr. Stratton of Mullica Hill in a Mercer. Green won the race because he was lighter and Alcyon's sharp curves were hard for the Mercer to negotiate.

THE NORWOOD OUTING CLUB, C. 1909. There is not much information on the Norwood Outing Club. Alcyon Park was used as a meeting place for such camping clubs. Note the uniformed gentleman in both of these real photo postcards.

ALCYON SPEEDWAY, LABOR DAY OF 1938. Hank Rogers is driving Bill Drake's Ford sprint car. Rogers won his first main event feature on this day. He went on to be one of sprint car's best. This photograph is from a glass negative.

THE HOUSE OF DAVID BASEBALL TEAM, 1938. This traveling Jewish ball team visited the Alcyon Park ball field many times during the 1930s. On July 1, 1938, the team was beaten by the Alcyon All-Star team by a score of 6-1. Alcyon Park played host to many of the Negro League teams and to Connie Mack's Philadelphia Athletics.

BILL VAIL'S NO. 1 SPRINT CAR. Bill Vail (right) was the Alcyon Speedway promoter from 1935 until 1960. He is shown here with Jim Weir. Tony Bone drove this car in 1937. Bone set fast time at Hatfield, Pennsylvania, on September 11, 1937.

JEWEL VAIL'S NO. 25 SPRINT CAR, C. THE 1940S. Local driver Lew Mood is shown at Alcyon Speedway sitting in the sprint car owned by Jewel Vail, wife of Bill Vail. The car is said to be the first owned by a woman in the United States. Lew Mood was the 1957 track sportsman champion, driving a stock car at Alcyon Speedway.

ALCYON SPEEDWAY, AUGUST 28, 1946. Driver Crocky Wright (No. 3) of Philadelphia, Pennsylvania¡, charges down the homestretch at the start of the race. Note that the flagman started the races on the track.

ALCYON SPEEDWAY, JULY 4, 1946. In the front row are Buster Williams (left) and Jack McNeal. The second row includes Walt Walker (right).

GENE POWELL'S SPRINT CAR, 1941. Sprint car races were held at Alcyon Speedway on holidays during the summer and during the annual Gloucester County Grange Fair. Gene Powell was a local owner and attended the races frequently.

PACKED GRANDSTANDS AT ALCYON SPEEDWAY, JULY 4, 1946. This picture is unique because it shows track promoter Bill Vail (see arrow) sitting in the stands with race fans. Auto racing was very popular in the 1940s and 1950s.

ALCYON SPEEDWAY, JULY 4, 1946. This photograph shows the start of the sprint car race before a packed grandstand. To the left, a starter stands on the track.

A MIKE MAGILL AUTOGRAPHED PICTURE, MAY 31, 1954. Mike Magill was from Haddonfield and drove sprint cars and stock cars at Alcyon Speedway. Magill raced at the Indianapolis 500 in the late 1950s. He was a United Racing Club champion in 1950 and 1951. In 1953, he was co-champion with Charles Miller. He was also Alcyon Speedway's 1951 modified champion.

BILL VAIL'S NO. 1 SPRINT CAR, 1937. The car is shown gassing up at Prosser & Johnson's on West Jersey Avenue. Sprint cars traveled the East Coast to visit different tracks, usually on holidays and during county fairs.

THE ALCYON SPEEDWAY PIT AREA, LABOR DAY 1946. Not everyone enjoyed the sprint cars at Alcyon Speedway. In this view, Johnny Rhoda of Gloucester City cries away as his father takes the photograph.

THE LUCKY TETER THRILL SHOW, 1941. The Lucky Teter Thrill Show was one of the earliest to visit Alcyon Speedway, along with B. Ward Beam, Joie Chitwood, and Ken Butler. The shows drew large crowds and were very popular. This photograph shows Lucky about to miss his landing. He returned later in the year to successfully complete the jump. The picture is autographed to the track financial officer, Tom Sawyer.

JOIE CHITWOOD, SPRINT CAR DRIVER, 1945. In this photograph, taken at the speedway in Trenton, Joie Chitwood (No. 2) and Bill Holland (No. 15) race side by side on the dirt track. Chitwood started in sprint cars and finished doing thrill shows.

ALCYON SPEEDWAY, 1950. The Joie Chitwood Auto Daredevils visited Alcyon Speedway often. Chitwood was joined by C. Ward Beam, Lucky Teter, Lucky Lee Crosby, and Ken Butler. Thrill shows were very popular at the track.

JOIE CHITWOOD, c. 1950. Joie Chitwood was a sprint car driver, track promoter, and event coordinator during the heyday of auto racing. He started his thrill show later in life, and his sons still tour the country with the Joie Chitwood Thrill Show.

BILL VAIL'S BACKYARD, C. THE 1940S. Bill Vail chained his racecar to a tree to keep the children from pushing it down the alley. Pictured are his son Herb Vail (left) and friend Dave Horner.

BERT BROOKS, MAY 31, 1954. Bert Brooks, United Racing Club champion in 1954, 1956, 1957, and 1958, is shown sitting in his No. 4 sprint car at Alcyon Speedway. He was quite a fan favorite and won races all along the East Coast with the United Racing Club.

JOE SZABO IN CAR NO. 32, MAY 31, 1954. This is another of the United Racing Club driver photographs taken at Alcyon Speedway. The United Racing Club decal is shown on the side of the car.

WIMPY ERVIN IN CAR NO. 24, MAY 31, 1954. Note Ervin's driving uniform and the cigar in his mouth. This photograph also shows the ball field, grandstands, and lighting system in the background.

CARL BECKER IN CAR NO. 7, MAY 31, 1954. This photograph shows the pit area of Alcyon Speedway. The grandstands were used for the ball field in the infield of the track. Carl Becker was a United Racing Club driver and traveled with the club to various tracks along the East Coast.

ALCYON SPEEDWAY, JULY 4, 1946. This beautiful racing photograph was taken from the track. It shows the close proximity of the race fans to the track. The drivers did not wear special clothing and cars did not have roll bars during this period of racing.

DRIVER BOB COONEY IN CAR NO. 8, MAY 31, 1954. Another of the United Racing Club's more notable drivers, Bob Cooney was a crowd favorite at the Alcyon Track and was often a front runner.

NORMAN "POP" BAY IN CAR NO. 7. Norman Bay, a driver from Paulsboro, raced sprint cars and stock cars at Alcyon Speedway and along the East Coast during the 1940s and 1950s.

DRIVER LUCKY LUX IN CAR NO. 12, MAY 31, 1954. The United Racing Club sprint cars visited Alcyon Speedway often, and many drivers became famous in the early 1950s.

CHARLES STERN IN CAR NO. 43, MAY 31, 1954. Fitted with a long-sleeve shirt and a plastic helmet with leather straps, this driver is ready for a long day on the Alcyon dirt track.

Three

ALCYON PARK

PICNIC WAGONS, C. 1900. The second wagon from the left is lettered, "I.G. Cox & Bro. Builders." The two wagons to the right belong to H. Stanley & Sons of Westville.

THE PARKING AREA AT ALCYON PARK, C. 1900. The back field of Alcyon Park was used for parking. The lot, pictured when wagons were the transportation of the day, was a popular meeting place.

THE PARKING AREA AT ALCYON PARK, C. 1920. The invention of the automobile did not stop the people from coming to Pitman's Alcyon Park. This photograph shows many of the cars parked at Alcyon Park in the early 1900s.

SWIMMING AT ALCYON LAKE, 1910. One of Alcyon Park's main attractions was Alcyon Lake. During the summer, thousands of vacationers would come to Pitman's amusement park and lake. In this view, the lake is getting a lot of use.

ALCYON LAKE, 1910. Wool bathing suits were in style when Alcyon Lake became a meeting place in the early 1900s. This photograph shows many youngsters bathing while parents enjoy the shaded banks of the lake.

RIDE THE PRETZEL AT ALCYON PARK, 1940. This photograph shows one of Alcyon Park's most popular rides near the end of the park's activity in the early 1940s. The park became worn and in need of repair, as this picture shows. Once a great amusement park, Alcyon Park was torn down and Alcyon Lake became the main attraction until Alcyon Speedway became popular in the late 1940s.

THE TOBOGGAN RIDE, 1913. This was one of New Jersey's early roller coasters. It thrilled many visitors to Alcyon Park for more than 30 years.

ALCYON PARK, 1903. This view shows some of the participants in the 1903 C.M. Divine encampment at Alcyon Park. Alcyon Park was used often for religious retreats in the early 1900s.

A NORWOOD OUTING CLUB ENCAMPMENT, SUMMER 1909. Pictured is another example of camping at Alcyon Park. This real photo postcard shows members of the Norwood Outing Club in front of their tents.

ALCYON LAKE'S BOARDWALK, C. 1938. This unique photograph shows the bowling alley and boardwalk with Alcyon Lake drained. The lake may have been drained for cleaning, or the dam may have broken.

SPEEDBOAT RACES ON ALCYON LAKE, 1955. Races were part of the 50th-anniversary celebration. Note the Alcyon Lake billboard in the background by the Pitman Kiwanis Club.

ALCYON LAKE, C. THE 1940S. In the 1940s, the diving board was still on the dam on Holly Avenue. Boating was as popular as swimming at Alcyon Lake. Many residents held badges, sold by the Pitman Rotary Club, for swimming in the lake.

ALCYON LAKE, C. THE 1940S. The boardwalk from Holly Avenue to the amusement park had the low diving board. The expert board was on a platform offshore.

THE ALCYON PARK BOARDWALK, C. 1915. These two men have been caught by surprise by the photographer. The photograph shows the boardwalk and bowling alley out over the lake. The building straight ahead of the boardwalk is the bathhouse. On top of the hill, to the right, is the home of Mr. Wyne, the original owner of Wyne's Mill Pond (later Alcyon Lake). The theater stage is over the bowling alley.

THE ALCYON PARK FAIRGROUNDS, 1915. This postcard shows the midway during the Gloucester County Grange Fair. The fair was held annually at Alcyon Park during the summer.

Four

HISTORIC BUILDINGS

THE DILKS DRUGSTORE, C. 1920. The drugstore was located at the corner of Broadway and Pitman Avenue. Dilks had a soda fountain on the first floor and an amusement parlor on the second floor. This was the first business established in this residential block of downtown Pitman.

THE ROBBINS LUMBER AND MILLWORK BUILDING, 1940. The lumber-storage building shown in this picture was located across from Alcyon Lake on Holly Avenue. Some of the Robbins buildings were destroyed after a dam broke at Alcyon Lake and they were washed away. Peter Lumber now stands on this location.

THE GEORGE WASHINGTON CARR RESIDENCE, 1906. This house was located at Alcyon Lake. George Washington Carr and his brother Dr. Henry Carr owned Alcyon Park and Alcyon Track. This home was located where the Holly Court West Apartments entrance is now located. During the stock-car years at Alcyon Speedway, the cars would enter the road in front of George Washington Carr's home to get to the racetrack.

THE ROBLEYN HOME, BROADWAY, 1913. This home was owned by the H. Ridgely Robinson family. The photograph shows the home into which the Robinsons moved on November 17, 1913. The Pitman Manor now stands on the site.

THE PITMAN MASONIC CLUBHOUSE, C. THE 1920S. The Masonic clubhouse, located on the corner of Lincoln and McKinley Avenues, is shown decorated for the Fourth of July. The building was hit by fire in the 1950s and was rebuilt. The new building was razed in the 1980s, and houses were built in its place. The new Masonic Hall is on Lambs Road.

THE HOTEL PITMAN, PITMAN AVENUE, C. 1949. The Hotel Pitman, located on the corner of Pitman and Fernwood Avenues, was popular in the early 1900s as a meeting place and restaurant. The hotel is now occupied by weekly and full-time residents. It looks as it did when built in 1907 by S.B. Goff of Camden. Goff's medicines were famous all over the country, including his cough syrup.

THE PITMAN GOLF CLUB, 1930. The Pitman Golf Club, in Mantua Township, was built in 1927. It is now owned and operated by the Gloucester County Board of Chosen Freeholders. It is scheduled to be razed in 2002 to make room for a new clubhouse.

SUNSET AUDITORIUM, C. 1940. Sunset Auditorium is located on Laurel Avenue and was the only open-air movie in town. It was sponsored by the Pitman Cottagers' Association. Movies in the mid-1920s cost 25¢ for adults and 15¢ for children. The auditorium is still used today for concerts and community activities.

THE BROADWAY THEATER, C. THE 1930s. This photograph was taken from an original negative that was used for postcards. The Broadway Theater now has a different marquee, but the interior remains the same. The organ used for silent movies has been rebuilt and is used for special events today.

THE SUMMIT AVENUE SCHOOL, 1910. The school was built in 1909 with eight rooms. Within two years, it was necessary to add four more rooms. The building served Pitman for 62 years. It was torn down in 1972.

PITMAN HIGH SCHOOL. Pitman High School was built in 1923, with L. Arthur Walton as principal. Located on Holly Avenue, it became the middle school in 1970.

Five

DOWNTOWN PITMAN

A HORSE AND BUGGY ON BROADWAY, C. 1900. To the left is the Knights of the Golden Eagle Hall, which was built in 1890. To the right is the C.H. Kline Barber Shop. Note the old barber pole in the street and the sale of cigars and tobacco. In the front is a horse and wagon and "Scott's Accommodations."

BROADWAY FROM PITMAN AVENUE, LOOKING NORTH, C. THE 1920S. Shown on this postcard are the Dilks drugstore, on the corner, and automobiles lining Broadway. Dust was a real problem for the merchants of the day.

THE BILL OWENS SUNOCO STATION, 1957. This station was located next to the post office on Broadway and Arbutus Avenue. Bill Owens moved to the other end of town and opened a Gulf station while this location changed oil companies, with Getty being the last to pump gas. It is now an automotive repair center.

54

THE PITMAN WELCOME SIGN IN BALLARD PARK, C. THE 1940S. This sign is located at Broadway and Pitman Avenue. The Philadelphia bus stop of the G.R. Wood Company was used until the 1970s. It is now located at the other end of Ballard Park on Broadway.

THE PITMAN TRUST COMPANY, C. THE 1930S. The building is located on Broadway between Pitman Avenue and Theater Avenue. It is no longer a bank but is in use as a tax preparer's office.

BROADWAY WHEN IT WAS A DIRT ROAD, 1915. Broadway was paved in 1920. Pitman National Bank is to the left. It was built in June 1911 of Holmsburg granite, and the nine-ton vault had to be moved on rollers from the freight office. George Washington Carr was the first president of the bank, and the first day's deposits totaled $32,086.69. The post office to the right was built in 1908. The Dilks drugstore of is on the right side of the road on the corner.

THE BOROUGH OF PITMAN HONOR ROLL, C. THE 1950S. The honor roll was dedicated to the local men and women who served their country in World War II. It was located at the entrance to First Avenue.

THE PITMAN HOUSE. This is the Sunday dinner menu at the Pitman House, which was located on the corner of Broadway and Holly Avenue. The Harker family owned the establishment from 1913 to 1923, and it was known then as the Harker House.

Special Dinner
SUNDAY
At the Pitman House
Broadway and Holly Avenue
PITMAN, N. J.

E. ADAMS, Proprietor

...Menu...

CHICKEN NOODLE SOUP
BROILED CHICKEN WITH BACON
OR
SMALL TENDER STEAK
CORN FRITTERS   GREEN PEAS
MASHED POTATOES
WALDORF SALAD   ICE CREAM
COFFEE

Oysters, Steaks, Chops?
Yes, we have them.

CANDIES   CIGARS   ICE CREAM

THE PITMAN POST OFFICE, 1908. This postcard shows one of Pitman's first post offices not in the Pitman Grove area. It was located on Broadway at the southwest corner of First Avenue. This building was replaced with one located at Broadway and Second Avenue that is now the Pitman News Agency building.

57

PITMAN NATIONAL BANK, 1913. The building, located on Broadway at First Avenue, still stands today but it is no longer a bank. It was an architectural masterpiece when it was built. This real photo postcard was mailed on March 14, 1913.

WOOLWORTH'S FIVE-AND-DIME, C. THE 1950S. Woolworth's was a real staple for small towns from the 1940s to the 1960s. Built in 1936, the Woolworth store in Pitman served residents for many years before closing in the 1970s. Today, this building is the police station and borough hall.

BROADWAY, LOOKING NORTH FROM PITMAN AVENUE, C. 1945. This is a good view of Pitman National Bank and Trust Company's original clock. Note the tin roofs over the sidewalks, with both A & P and Acme markets on Broadway.

HARMON DILKS JR.'S DRUGSTORE, C. 1900. Located at Broadway and Pitman Avenue, this building has been a retail business for more than 100 years. The real photo postcard shows it as the H. Dilks Jr. drugstore, with a Breyers ice cream sign and a small roadside sign. The store is now Bob's Hobbies and Crafts.

THE RAILROAD CROSSING AT BROADWAY NEAR LAUREL AVENUE, 1945. Note the crossing guard in front of his shelter. The sign on the building reads, "No loafing in or around the watch box."

THE PITMAN RAILROAD STATION, 1906. This postcard shows the train station in the early 1900s, when more than 10,000 commuters would arrive during the summer months to attend the Methodist Camp Meeting Association services in Pitman Grove.

THE PITMAN TRAIN STATION, 1901. Pitman was an extremely busy station in the early 1900s. Rail travel was in its heyday, and Pitman was part of it.

THE PITMAN TRAIN STATION, 1912. This picture was taken from a glass negative. The area around the station was a very busy part of town. Note both automobiles and horse-drawn wagons. Buses are also present near the electric pole.

BROADWAY, LOOKING NORTH, 1912. This is Broadway just north of the railroad crossing. Pitman National Bank is to the left. There were houses instead of businesses on Broadway. The street is lined with cars.

THE WELCOME SIGN IN BALLARD PARK, C. 1916. This sign greeted the people coming to the Gloucester County Grange Fair. Passengers from the train to Broadway had to pass under the arch.

BILL LAWS, BOOTBLACK FOR KIRCHNER'S SHAVING PARLOR, 1918. The parlor, located on Pitman Avenue, was purchased in 1926 by Joe Mangano and renamed Joe's Barber Shop. In 1950, the shop moved to its present-day location at 146 South Broadway. The shop is still in the Mangano family more than 75 years later.

A FIRST AVENUE BARBERSHOP, 1898. This shop was located at Broadway and First Avenue on the site of the present-day bank building owned by A.A. Williams. It boasted three barbers with no waiting.

THE SODA FOUNTAIN IN THE DILKS DRUGSTORE, 1913. This soda fountain was located on the corner of Broadway and Pitman Avenue. The building is now Bob's Hobbies and Crafts.

THE INTERIOR OF THE BROADWAY THEATER, 1932. This postcard of the interior of the Broadway Theater offers a good view of the balcony and the decorative ceiling.

BROADWAY, LOOKING NORTH FROM PITMAN AVENUE, 1951. This was a wonderful era for small towns, as shown in this view of a busy downtown.

MERRITT'S HOUSE OF FLOWERS, 1940. Merritt's is located on the corner of Broadway and Laurel Avenue. The Merritt family has served Pitman for more than 70 years.

THE FOURTH OF JULY PARADE, C. THE 1950S. The Fourth of July has always been a big day in Pitman. Note the F.W. Woolworth five-and-dime and the Dorman's Sporting Goods store in the background.

TRIO MOTORS, C. 1960. Trio Motors was located at 530 South Broadway. It was advertised as Gloucester County's oldest Ford agency. The house to the right still stands today.

THE JOHN S. STRATTON PONTIAC DEALERSHIP, C. 1960. The Stratton dealership was at the North Broadway location from 1941 to the mid-1970s.

THE PITMAN POST OFFICE, C. 1940. The post office was built in 1935–1936. It is located on North Broadway at Hazel Avenue. The modern facility is still in use today.

PITMAN AVENUE FROM SIMPSON AVENUE TO BROADWAY, 1910. This is a great photograph of the businesses along Pitman Avenue. Note the Pitman Grove Arch at Broadway.

THE WHITE STAR LAUNDRY, 1948. The White Star Laundry entrance was located on West Jersey Avenue. The laundry building ran along Grandview Avenue to Oakcrest Avenue.

BROADWAY, LOOKING SOUTH, 1906. Horses and buggies were used on the dirt road in the early 1900s. The large building to the left with the unique windows is the S.P. Clark Building.

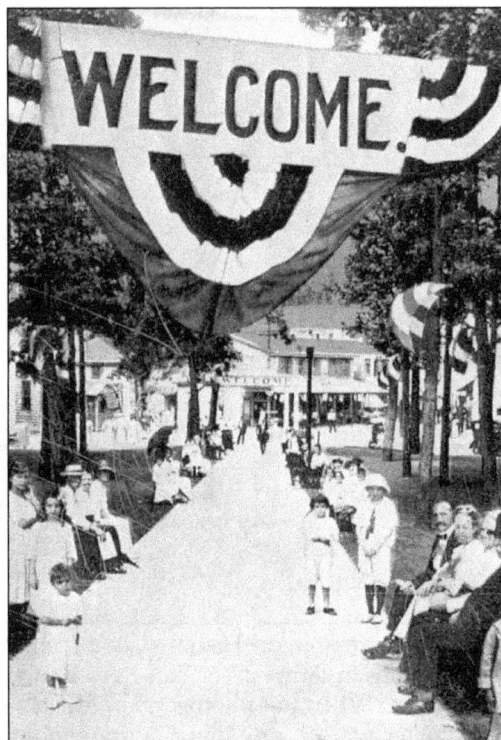

PILGRIMS PATHWAY, BALLARD PARK, c. 1905. The walkway leading from the Pitman train station to Broadway is lined with visitors to Pitman. At the far end is the welcome arch at the corner of Pitman Avenue and Broadway. This pathway cut through Ballard Park, in downtown Pitman.

THE PITMAN NATIONAL BANK AND TRUST COMPANY. This building is located on Broadway where Pitman Avenue starts. The building still stands today but is no longer used as a bank. The old town clock has been replaced with a more modern one.

THE INTERSECTION OF HOLLY AVENUE AND BROADWAY, 1954. This is one of the busiest intersections in Pitman. You can go to Richwood, Barnsboro, Glassboro, or Delsea Drive from this corner. When this photograph was taken, the old gas station sign still stood on the corner. Parking meters were also in use during this era.

Six

CHURCHES

THE PITMAN METHODIST CHURCH, C. 1906. The first church in Pitman organized in 1885 with 43 charter members of the Methodist Episcopal Church. This church is located on the corner of Broadway and Holly Avenue.

THE PITMAN METHODIST CHURCH, C. 1970. This view from Holly Avenue shows the Pitman Methodist Church. Over the years, many renovations and additions converted the original building into what is shown here.

THE METHODIST CHURCH INTERIOR, C. 1942. The altar, pictured at Christmastime, shows the beauty of the season.

LOT
on North Broadway, adjoining the present church, has
been secured as a site
FOR
a new church and Sunday School building; and there
are now for
SALE
9000 square feet of land at 30 cents a square foot to
be donated to the
PITMAN BAPTIST CHURCH

? I hereby pledge to buy .300. square feet, to be paid .... in cash and
.... per month before December 1, 1921. (Squares to be punched out as paid.)
Name Earnest worker Address..............................

THE PITMAN BAPTIST CHURCH, 1921. This unique postcard was used to raise money for the Church Building Fund. The money was used to purchase land for an addition to the existing church building.

THE FIRST BAPTIST CHURCH OF PITMAN, 1955. The addition is shown being built by the Schneeman Builders. Located on North Broadway, the church was started in 1909.

PITMAN'S FIRST BAPTIST CHURCH, EASTER 1945. Located on North Broadway, the church has gone through many changes over the years and will celebrate its 100th anniversary in 2009.

OUR LADY QUEEN OF PEACE ROMAN CATHOLIC CHURCH. This church is located on the corner of Pitman Avenue and Highland Terrace. The church was built in 1950 and was dedicated in April 1951.

74

THE CHRISTIAN AND MISSIONARY ALLIANCE CHURCH, 1952. Members of the Sunday school class of Erma Garrison (back) pose on the lawn of the church. From left to right are David Owens, Patricia DuBois, an unidentified girl, and Ralph Richards Jr.

THE CHRISTIAN AND MISSIONARY ALLIANCE CHURCH, 1996. This church was built in October 1927 and was dedicated on March 11, 1928. The building is still used as a church, but the Christian and Missionary congregation built a new church outside of Pitman.

THE FIRST PRESBYTERIAN CHURCH, C. 1930. The original church building was constructed in 1925 and was dedicated in 1926. The church is located on South Broadway between Crafton and Wildwood Avenues.

THE FIRST PRESBYTERIAN CHURCH, C. 1970. This photograph shows the additions made to the original 1925 building.

76

THE INTERIOR OF THE FIRST PRESBYTERIAN CHURCH, C. 1942. This view of the Presbyterian altar has a stained-glass window as a center of attention. The altar is adorned with flowers and evergreens and makes for a serene setting for parishioners to enjoy.

THE CHURCH OF THE NAZARENE. The Church of the Nazarene was organized in 1952. The church edifice was built on the corner of North Broadway and Evergreen Avenue.

THE CHURCH OF THE GOOD SHEPHERD, C. **1920.** The Episcopal church was built in 1907 at the corner of Wildwood Avenue and Highland Terrace. Since that time, additions to the church were built in 1950 and in 1964.

THE CHURCH OF THE GOOD SHEPHERD, C. **1940.** This interior photograph shows the altar and the original block building wall.

Seven

THE POLICE AND
FIRE DEPARTMENTS

FIRE COMPANY NO. 2, 1905. Fire Company No. 2 was located on Fourth Avenue in Pitman Grove. Founded in 1897, it disbanded in 1923. A.H. Moses was the chief and founder. He later belonged to Pitman Fire Patrol.

THE WRECK OF ENGINE NO. 1987, JANUARY 31, 1906. This Pennsylvania Railroad engine was built in Altoona, Pennsylvania, in 1901. The boiler explosion occurred on Monday, January 31, 1906, between Lambs Road and Holly Avenue in Pitman. The engineer was injured and eventually returned to work. The fireman and head brakeman were killed.

THE PITMAN POLICE DEPARTMENT, 1955. From left to right are the following: (front row) Paul Maass (clerk), C. Jay Mounts (clerk), Allen Weisel, Robert Black (special officer), Earl Young, and Herschel Luce; (back row) Oran Lloyd, William Hampton, George Hausmann (chief), Oscar Stiles, E.J. Williams (clerk), and Kenneth Austin.

PITMAN FIRE PATROL, SEPTEMBER 21, 1905. This piece of fire apparatus was built to the specifications of W.C.K. Walls. It was the first to carry ladder, bell, lantern, and hose. The apparatus was stored under the Lizzie Smith Temple until 1906.

PITMAN FIRE PATROL, 1908. Pitman Fire Patrol members were proud to show off their newest firefighting equipment to the residents of Pitman Grove in the early 1900s.

PITMAN FIRE PATROL FIREFIGHTING EQUIPMENT AND MEMBERS, 1906. These two photographs show the early firefighting brigade in front of the firehouse. It is clear from these pictures that the Pitman Grove area was well protected in the early years.

PITMAN FIRE PATROL, AUGUST 18, 1906. From left to right are the following: (front row) ? Southwood, Jasper Perry, Robert Fadley, Edgar Thompson (mascot), John Thompson, Arthur Toland, and John Stehr; (middle row) Ed Judd, Charles Poole, George Gallagher Sr., Harry McBurney, W.C.K. Walls, Walter Bowen, and George Hannum; (back row) George Ellick, W. Gebhardsbaur, L. Lupton, Al Peterson, Al Walton, George Gallagher, H. Whitehead, ? Wilber, ? Stalcup, Tony Cambell, Johnson Simmington, and Dave Supplee.

THE PITMAN FIRE PATROL FIREHOUSE, 1906. This photograph shows the fire building without people or fire equipment. It was quite a building for this time period and shows the importance of a fire company in the Pitman Grove area.

FIRE COMPANY NO. 1, C. 1910. Fire Company No. 1 was formed in 1901, and the station was built on Simpson Avenue. The land was purchased for $600. The president was Thomas Goodwin, and the vice president was Elmer D. Crane.

FIRE COMPANY NO. 1, 1928. This photograph shows the fire company's equipment parked in front of the firehouse and the borough hall. The firehouse and borough hall were attached and were located on Broadway north of Holly Avenue.

THE PITMAN MUNICIPAL BUILDING, C. THE 1940S. This building was constructed in 1890 by the Knights of the Golden Eagle. It was sold to the borough in 1921 as the new borough hall. It was later used as a fire company and library. Today, it is a privately owned physical therapy office.

THE HIGHLAND CHEMICAL ENGINE COMPANY, SEPTEMBER 15, 1940. From left to right are Martin Ewe (chief), Clifton Boyce (driver), ? Albright, Arthur Euler, Harry Lang, Clinton Kandle Jr., Everett Harbison, Edward Evans, Ambrose Schrader, John Hasher, and H. Leonard Eckman.

SECOND ALARMERS, 1949. The Highland Chemical Engine Company was famous for its Second Alarmers comic brigade. Second Alarmers are shown passing Merritt's House of Flowers and Woodward's Auto Parts on Broadway. Merritt's House of Flowers, located on the corner of South Broadway and Laurel Avenue, is still in business today.

THE HIGHLAND CHEMICAL ENGINE COMPANY, C. 1960. From left to right are the following: (front row) Bob Shirley, Roy Davis, Paul Schoff, Bud Bogia, Bud Mitton, Edward Stackenwalt, Fred Genter, and Harold Ewe; (middle row) Harold Mathis, Bob Thren, Ray Hamilton, Glenn Shirley, Howard Carter, Len Eckman, Scott Anderson, George Guenther, and Bill Avis; (back row) Arch Murphy, John Collier, Fred Genter Sr., Al Leiby, Jack Kelley, Wayne Groff, Clint Carter, Norman Murphy, ? Campbell, George Kelly, Bob Cressman Sr., John Fleming, Bill Sheldon, Hal Mitten, Ed Wickland, Earl Curry, Joe Young, Bill Thompson, and Harry VanDexter.

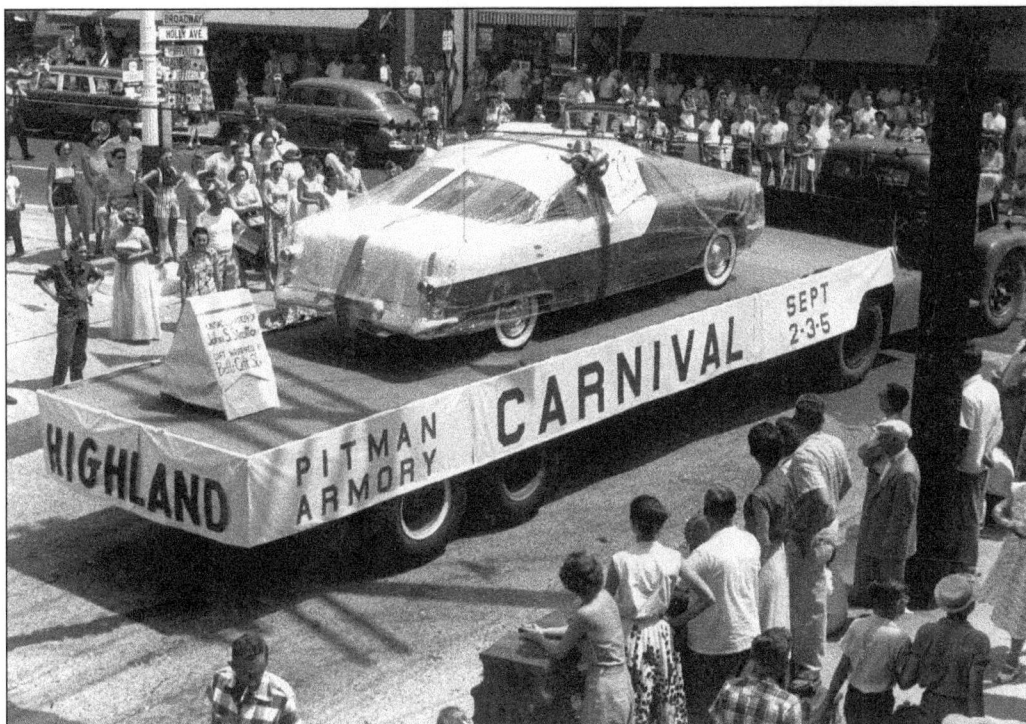

THE HIGHLAND CHEMICAL ENGINE COMPANY FLOAT, JULY 4, 1955. This photograph shows Highland's annual car for raffle from the John S. Stratton Pontiac dealership in Pitman. The car was on the float during the 50th-anniversary parade. It is approaching Broadway on Holly Avenue.

THE HIGHLAND CHEMICAL ENGINE COMPANY CAR, C. 1961. From left to right are Pontiac dealer John S. Stratton, Highland member Glenn Shirley, and Jim Hunter. The picture was taken in front of the Stratton dealership on North Broadway.

87

SECOND ALARMERS, C. THE 1950s. Highland's famous comic brigade toured the mid-Atlantic coast firemen's parade circuit and was a trophy winner many times. From left to right (above) are Scott Anderson (on the ladder), Ossie Osborn, Bill Fuller, Clint Carter, Vernon Dunn, Sid Howarth, Tom Stores, N. Carter, Robert Rudolph, Frank Nester, and unidentified. The photograph below shows the comic brigade in action.

Eight

ALCYON SPEEDWAY

AN AERIAL VIEW OF ALCYON SPEEDWAY, 1952. Alcyon Speedway was known for its unique five-turn shape. It was one of the most difficult tracks to drive and the most rewarding if you won. It drew the most popular and talented drivers of its time. The stock cars raced from 1948 until 1960, when the track closed. Alcyon Lake is in the front, and the Pitman Fire Patrol parking lot is in the upper right.

DRIVER GEORGIE MOORE AND CREW IN THE VICTORY LANE, 1954. This photograph shows, from left to right, George Wingate, Sonny Dornberger, George Getz, Georgie Moore (driver), and Dutch Maulk (car owner). They are celebrating a feature win at Alcyon Speedway. George Wingate was an owner and promoter at Bridgeport Speedway in New Jersey from the 1970s to the 1990s. Sonny Dornberger became a legend as an engine builder up until his passing in the late 1990s.

ALCYON SPEEDWAY, C. THE 1950s. This is one of Alcyon Speedway's most spectacular wrecks. Driver Mel Verona walked away from the accident.

MEL VERONA'S HOMESTRETCH WRECK, C. THE 1950S. Rescue personnel rush to extract driver Mel Verona from this homestretch crash involving many cars. Although Verona escaped injury, driver Wild Bill Smith was injured and hospitalized. Smith died of pneumonia a few weeks later.

MEL VERONA AND HIS WRECKED CAR, C. THE 1950S. Mel Verona, uninjured and glad about it, is shown standing next to his uprighted car. Considering the condition of his car, it is hard to believe he was not hurt.

ALCYON SPEEDWAY, LABOR DAY OF 1960. Racing down the short shoot between turns four and five are Bob Malzahn (No. SSS), Al Tasnady (No. 44), Vince Conrad (No. 9), and Jackie McLaughlin (No. 111).

THE ALCYON SPEEDWAY BANQUET, 1953. Driver Steve Elias (left) accepts his 1953 modified championship trophy from Pitman's Bud Emery. Emery was known for his program center column called "Around the Five Turnz."

ALCYON SPEEDWAY, JULY 4, 1960. Although he did not do well, Runt Harris of Trenton raced at the speedway in 1960. He drove legendary car owner Junie Dunlevy's No. 90 car. This photograph was autographed in 1995 by Dunlevy in his NASCAR race shop.

ALCYON SPEEDWAY, JULY 4, 1959. Four of Alcyon Speedway's favorite drivers are shown in this picture. They are Jackie McLaughlin (No. 026), Budd Olsen (No. 98), Al Tasnady (No. 2), and Glenn Guthrie (No. 118). How popular was Alcyon Speedway in the 1950s? Look at the cars in the infield parking lot.

ALCYON SPEEDWAY RACING, 1960. Shown in front of the scoring pagoda are Carl VanHorn (No. 659), Johnny Roberts (No. 7), and Budd Olsen (No. 98). These were three of Alcyon Speedway's famous drivers who chose to race here. These top drivers from the East Coast visited Alcyon on a regular basis.

HOBO BAND NIGHT, 1955. Feature winner Jackie McLaughlin (in checkered shirt) accepts a trophy from the Hobo Band.

THE ALCYON SPEEDWAY POINT WINNER, 1951. Mike Magill (left) accepts a trophy from promoter Bill Vail for the Eastern Stock Car Racing Association Trophy for his point championship in 1951.

THE ALCYON SPEEDWAY BANQUET, 1956. A yearly tradition of thanking the newsmen, radio commentators, television sportscasters, advertising men, and friends of the track was held at the Original Bookbinder's Restaurant in Philadelphia, Pennsylvania. Track promoter Bill Vail is standing next to the man holding the sign.

SPRINT CAR RACING, 1948. Large crowds and big car counts made sprint car racing at Alcyon Speedway a popular event. Shown here is the start of the feature race on July 4, 1948. Notice the packed grandstands. This event was sponsored by the Pitman Post of the Veterans of Foreign Wars.

A PHOTO FINISH AT ALCYON SPEEDWAY, SEPTEMBER 26, 1958. This image shows Thorofare's Jackie McLaughlin (No. 026) and Bob Malzahn of Florida (No. SSS) in a photo finish. The win was given to Malzahn. The scorekeeper told photographer Bob Sweeten to rip up the photograph if it showed McLaughlin winning. Use your own judgment.

ALCYON SPEEDWAY AWARD WINNERS, SEPTEMBER 20, 1957. Being honored, from left to right, are Harry and Roy Batchelor for 25 years of flagging, announcer Bill Gregory for service, Bud Emery for public relations, promoter Bill Vail, and Matt Goukas of radio station WPEN.

THE ENTRANCE TO THE ALCYON SPEEDWAY PITS, 1959. A Pitman police officer controls traffic to the infield for stock-car entrants and fans. The entrance crossed over the track at the fifth turn and led to the infield parking and pit area from Track Avenue. Today, the entrance to Alcyon Park is located at the same area of Track Avenue.

RACING AT ALCYON SPEEDWAY, LABOR DAY 1960. Two of the East Coast's best drivers—Wil Cagle (No. 2) and Carl VanHorn (No. 659)—race each other down the backstretch at Alcyon Speedway. Wil Cagle came up from Florida during the summer to race at the Northeast dirt tracks.

AN ALCYON SPEEDWAY STOCK-CAR LINEUP, 1960. A heat race lines up at the start line at Alcyon Speedway. Included in this picture are drivers Johnny Flake in Joe Merlino's No. 104 and driver Bill Wark in Tom Raymer's No. 10a. Tom Raymer also owned No. 11, driven by Bob Becker.

AUTOGRAPH SEEKERS AT ALCYON SPEEDWAY, C. 1957. These two photographs show the Lyons family children collecting autographs from Jackie McLaughlin (above) and his brother-in-law Budd Olsen (right). After the races, fans would often search out their favorite drivers and get autographs. In these photographs, the pit area is full of fans.

JACKIE MCLAUGHLIN AND HIS NO. 300 CAR, 1957. This car was sponsored by a Vineland tractor dealer and a Forrest Grove used car parts owner. Although it had some success at Alcyon Speedway, it won the modified championship at the speedway in Flemington in the late 1950s.

ALCYON SPEEDWAY DREW MANY NASCAR DRIVERS. One of the first Southern invaders to Alcyon Speedway was Glen "Fireball" Roberts. He was said to have had a few run-ins with Trenton driver Chick DiNatale in the early 1950s.

ALCYON SPEEDWAY, 1950. Another NASCAR driver, Red Byron, visited Alcyon Speedway in the late 1940s and early 1950s.

ALCYON SPEEDWAY, 1951. Frank Munday was another of the NASCAR drivers to visit Alcyon Speedway. Note the driving uniform Munday used.

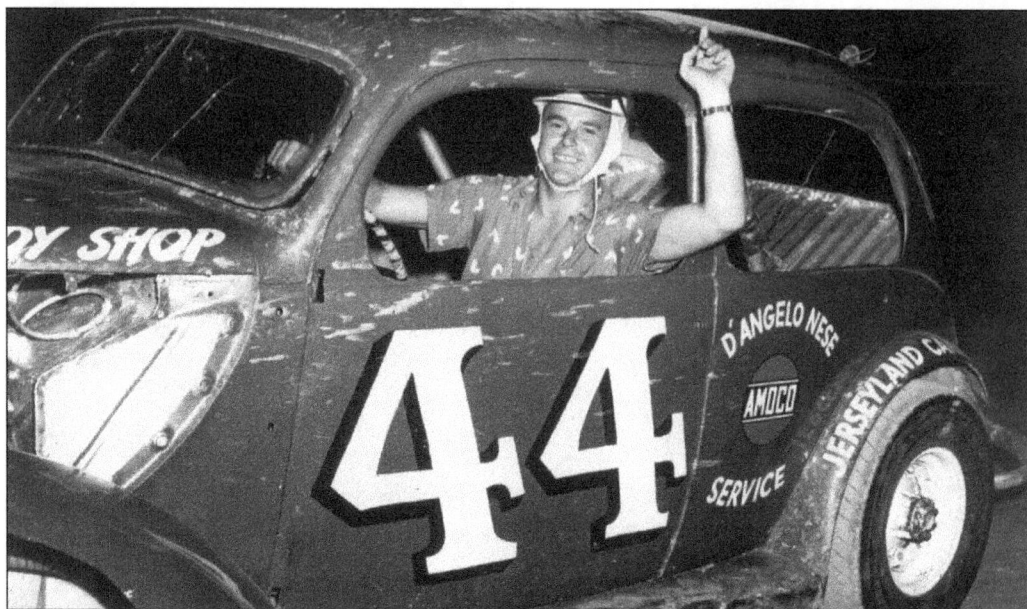

LOCAL FAN FAVORITE AL TASNADY, 1957. Although Al Tasnady of Vineland never won a championship at Alcyon Speedway, he held the track record of seven straight modified feature wins. Tasnady won at the Vineland Speedway often and was track champion there. He is shown in the No. 44 car of Neal Williams, a longtime stock-car owner from Vineland.

THE EASTERN STOCK CAR RACING ASSOCIATION BANQUET, 1953. From left to right are the following: (front row) two unidentified men, Elmer Auer, Steve Elias (modified champion), and Lew Mood; (middle row) Haig Avakian, Bill Hill, Don Battalini, unidentified, and Mel Verona; (back row) George Stockinger and unidentified. This racing association raced at Alcyon Speedway and Pleasantville Speedway for a club championship.

ALCYON SPEEDWAY RACING ACTION, 1952. This photograph of Alcyon Speedway's third turn shows driver Johnny Karp in the Beach Brothers No. 1 car racing with driver Lew Mood in the No. 29 car, sponsored by Rishel's Auto Body Shop in Pitman. Both drivers became track champions during their careers at Alcyon Speedway.

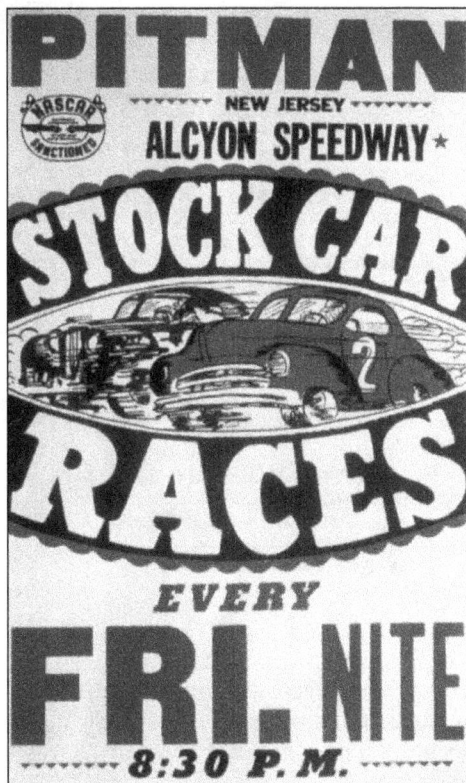

AN ALCYON SPEEDWAY ADVERTISEMENT POSTER, 1955. Alcyon Speedway was operated as a NASCAR track from 1955 until it closed in 1960. Placed on buildings and poles along the main roadway during that time period, these posters are very collectible today.

MOTORCYCLE RACES
PITMAN SPEEDWAY

SATURDAY SEPTEMBER 7th
1946

AMA SANCTION No. 9797

Supervision of

Luck Roamers MC
Vineland, N. J.

CLUB OFFICERS

PRESIDENT .... JOHN GOSS
VICE PRESIDENT .... PHIL BUZZA
SECRETARY . ..... MOTT. SACHETTI
TREASURER .... EARL EPLEY
REFEREE .... JOHN VARESIO

Twin Rockets MC
Aura, N. J.

CLUB OFFICERS

PRESIDENT .... HERBERT BOLD
VICE PRESIDENT . JAMES HENNESSY
SECRETARY ...... WALTER REEDER
TREASURER ..... LLOYD HERITAGE
REFEREE .... RAY BROWN

AMA OFFICIALS IN CHARGE

AL WALTERS, Harrisburg, Pa. .... Starter and AMA Referee
PAUL SHATTUCK, Philadelphia, Pa. .... Announcer and Clerk of Course
HANK MILLER, Philadelphia, Pa. .... Timer
JOHN VERASIO .... Pit Steward
RAY BROWN .... Pit Steward

William Vail - Track Manager

AN ALCYON SPEEDWAY MOTORCYCLE PROGRAM, SEPTEMBER 7, 1946. This program shows club officials and members of the American Motorcycle Association (AMA). Bill Vail was the track manager. Nine races were held this day, with Jimmy Chann winning the 20-lap feature race.

ALCYON SPEEDWAY
PROGRAM OF SPRINT EVENTS

RACE OFFICIALS

JOE SWARTZ, Starter   GEORGE FISHER, Announcer

KERMIT ANSTAST, Timer   ...., Pit Steward

FIRST EVENT TIME TRIALS

Car No.	Driver	Address	Time
18	Ducky Phelman	Reading, Pa.	30.2
1	Phil Mortaman	Plainfield, N. J.	32.2
27	Russ Campbell	Allentown, Pa.	
8	Pop Ritter	Bethlehem, Pa.	
41	Pete McKeone	Chester, Pa.	32
28	Joe Gillo	Scranton, Pa.	
55	Jake Pickler	Bethlehem, Pa.	30.2
98	Frank Cook	Erlton, N. J.	
7	Count Vasey	Richmond, Va.	
29	Bill Gouse	Carlisle, Pa.	
94	Bob Arndt	Allentown, Pa.	
3	Buster Keller	Reading, Pa.	
9	Berny Seigfried	Middletown, Pa.	
10	Al Forbear	Portsmouth, Ohio	32
2	Joe Mullen	Allentown, Pa.	
19	Steve Markovitch	Hatboro, Pa.	32.6
8	Art Williams	Middletown, N. Y.	
5	Sam Mayberry	Tompson, Conn.	
2	Tom Markey	Syracuse, N. Y.	
7	Gus Grizzback	Binghampton, N. Y.	
14	Marty Goether	Mullica Hill, N. J.	
7	Pat Rooney	Paulsboro, N. J.	34.6
21	Adolph Schilling	Chester, Pa.	

An Alcyon Speedway Sprint Car Program, August 13, 1947. This program lists the drivers and some of the time trial results. Note the addresses on the drivers listed. This illustrates the popularity of sprint car racing and the draw that Alcyon Speedway had.

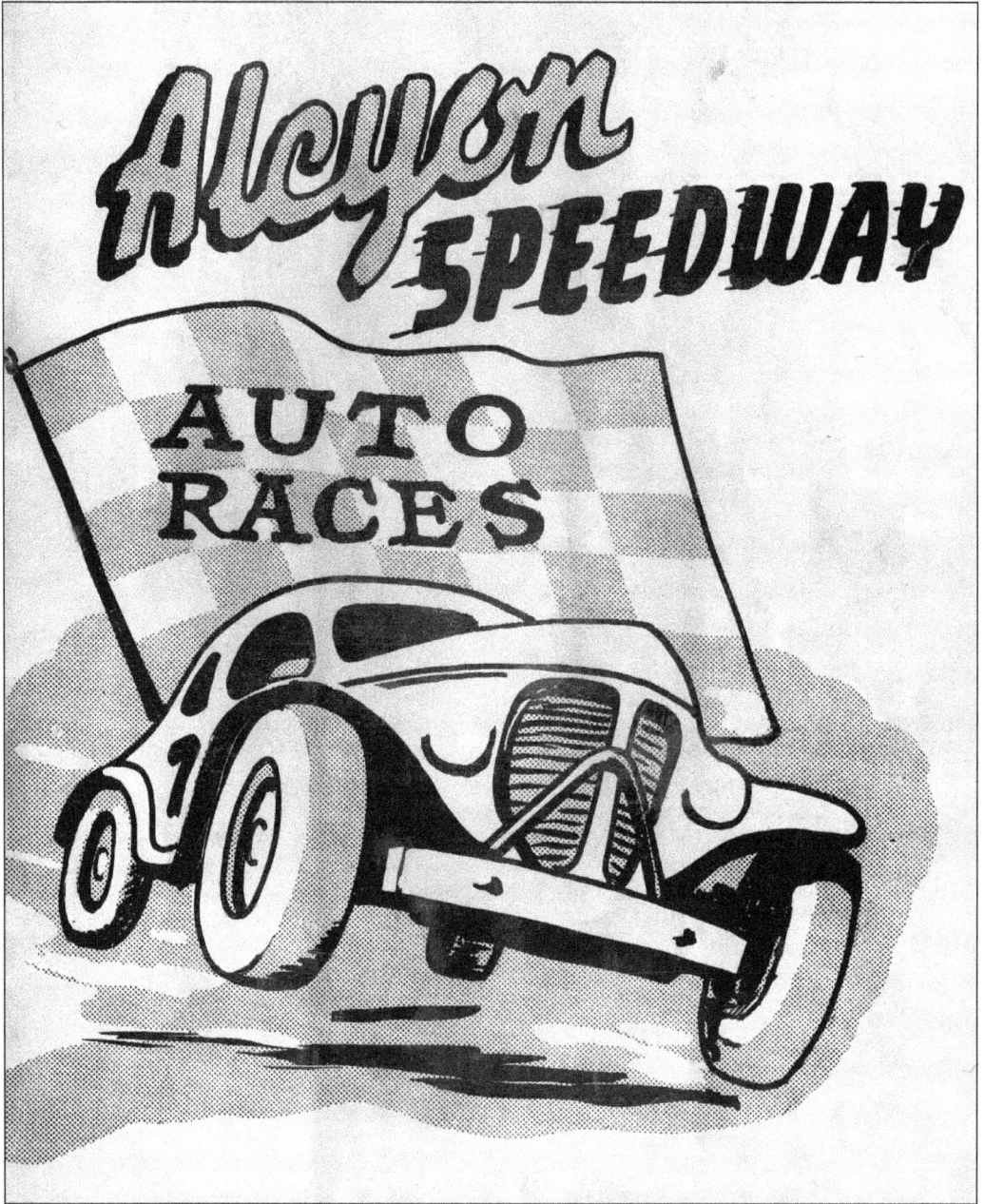

AN ALCYON SPEEDWAY RACING PROGRAM, 1956. This was the program cover used from 1953 to 1956. There has been no evidence of a program from the 1960 shortened race schedule. The program lists more than 75 drivers and has six racing photographs included.

AN ALCYON SPEEDWAY RACING PROGRAM, 1957. This program was an early one used until the end of the 1959 season. It contains eight pages for scoring and is full of local advertisements. Alcyon Speedway was one of the first tracks to produce a program of this quality. These programs were printed by Review Printing, which is still in business today.

A Nascar International Member Decal, 1957. The National Association of Stock Car Auto Racing (Nascar) supplied car owners and drivers with decals for their cars to race at a Nascar track. The decal had to be displayed.

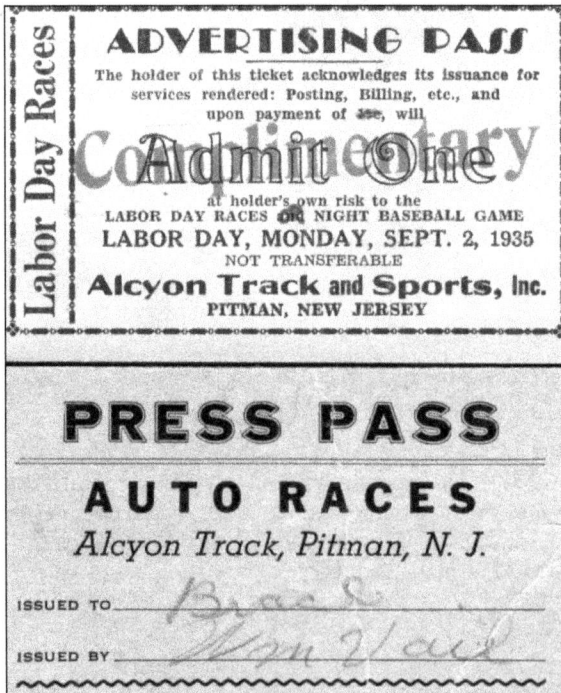

ALCYON SPEEDWAY RACE PASSES, 1935 AND 1940. To attract race fans to Alcyon Speedway, passes were often given to advertisers and press personnel to give away to friends and professional acquaintances. Shown here are two of these passes. One is from Labor Day of 1935, and the other is a press pass from 1940.

Alcyon Speedway Passes, 1941 and 1948. The 1941 pass was used to enter any race free throughout the season. The other, dated May 31, 1948, was a one-day pass. It is noted that the race was postponed.

1941 Season Pass

AUTO RACES

Alcyon Track, Pitman, N. J.

ISSUED TO ___Harrison Brace___

ISSUED BY ___Bill Vail___

ADVERTISING PASS

Auto Races - Alcyon Track

MAY 31ST, 1948

THIS TICKET ENTITLES HOLDER TO GENERAL ADMISSION AND BLEACHERS UPON PAYMENT OF SERVICE CHARGE PLUS TAX

postponed

GRANDSTAND No. 2 — T 4

AUTO RACES
ALCYON SPEEDWAY
PITMAN, N. J.

EVENT **1**

Estab. Price $1.00
Fed. Tax .20

TOTAL $1.20

ADMIT ONE

GLOBE TICKET COMPANY

HOLD THIS TICKET
NO MONEY REFUNDED

RAIN CHECK

Total Price $1.20

495

ALCYON SPEEDWAY — Row — Seat — EVENT 1 — T 4

GRANDSTAND No. 2

An Alcyon Speedway Ticket, 1958. This piece of Alcyon Speedway memorabilia is rare and sought after by collectors. The ticket is from the late 1950s and is in unused condition.

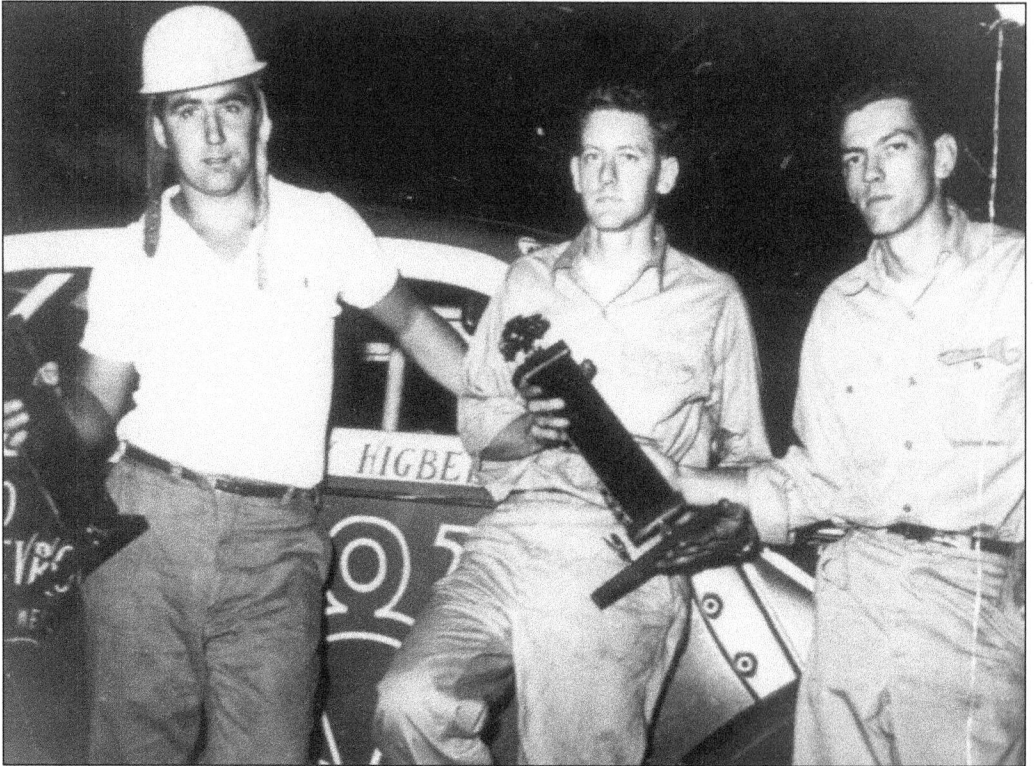

HOBBIE CAR RACING AT ALCYON SPEEDWAY, 1960. This photograph shows driver Bunky Higbee (left) and car owners Andy Ford (center) and Carl Ford in front of their V-8 numbered car. Higbee won the last Hobbie Feature race on Labor Day of 1960.

MODIFIED CAR RACING AT ALCYON SPEEDWAY, 1960. The No. 7 car shown here was driven by the 1960 and 1961 NASCAR modified champion Johnny Roberts of Baltimore, Maryland. Roberts drove this car to victory in the last modified feature held at Alcyon Speedway on Labor Day of 1960.

110

Nine

PEOPLE, PLACES, AND THINGS

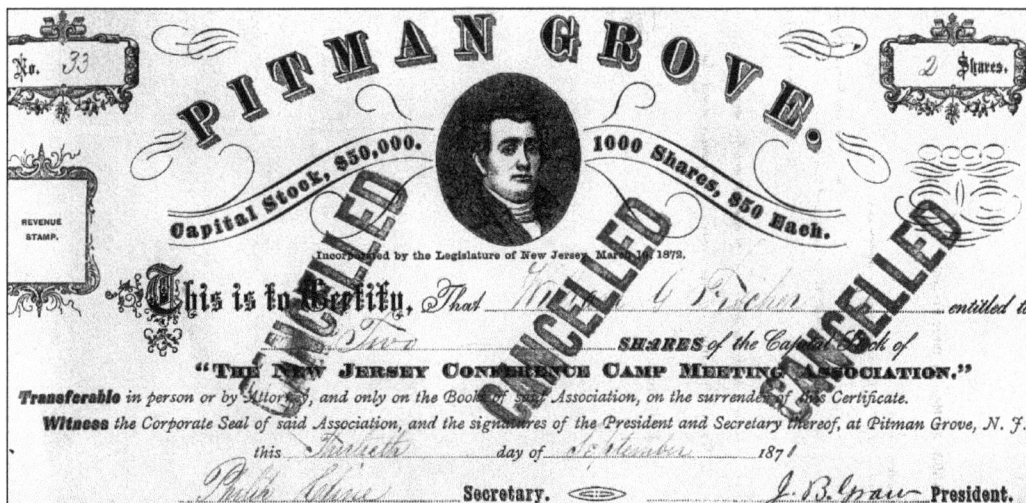

STOCK SHARES IN PITMAN GROVE. Two shares at $50 apiece were sold to William Fischer on September 13, 1871. One thousand shares were sold at $50 apiece, equaling $50,000.

Phiz

Class
of
1926

PHIZ, THE PITMAN HIGH SCHOOL YEARBOOK, 1926. The first graduating class dedicated this yearbook to Miss Zeigler and Mr. Hughes.

**A Pitman Cottagers' Association Booklet,
c. 1935.** Inside is a list of committees and trustees.
There is also an application for membership on the
back for $2.

"PITMAN PUTS PEP IN PEOPLE"

1900-1935

Pitman
Cottagers' Association
INCORPORATED

Pitman, N. J.

1935

MATTHEW KENNEY, President

HARRY E. BARNETT, Vice President

CHARLES W. LAMBERT, Treasurer

RUSSELL E. SWALM, Secretary

"Everybody Likes Pitman"

CLASS ROLL—EIGHTH GRADE

Addis, Grace	Horner, Roy	Park, Myra
Boltz, William	Hunter, Anna	Pomelear, Harry
Bostwick, Elberta	Hurley, Dorothy	Russell, Helen
Butcher, Allen	Jaggard, Eleanor	Scharnagle, George
Ceravolo, William	Krueger, Lawrence	Schoening, Edna
Clark, Amanda	Lapp, Marian	Schuh, Louise
Cliff, Shields	Lore, Frances	Shafer, Charles
Cossabone, George		Silver, Leon
Craig, Anna	MacFarland, Marian	Smiley, Robert
Croasdale, Eleanor	MacIntosh, Dorothy	Smith, Ruth
Croasdale, Helen	Magee, Vernon	Stanwood, Edward
Dall, Elizabeth	Maltman, William	Stroud, Grace
Davenport, Francis	Marr, Ethel	Somers, Vara
Ennis, Robert	Mayo, Harriet	Swab, William, Jr.
Euler, Charles	McCurdy, Oliver	
Euler, Raymond	McKay, Edith	Terry, Lillian
Fatkin, Donald	Mercer, Crystal	Titus, Addellmah
Gallagher, Ruth	Mole, Sara	Van Mater, Maude
Heim, Mildred	Moore, Betty	Wes coat, Russell
Hitchner, Thornton	Morris, Ruth	White, Francis
Horner, Delia	Murphy, Roy	Wilkins, Janet

FACULTY

S. MARGARET GRIM	MRS. LOUISE M. LAPP
MRS. HAZEL M. MYERS	MABEL LAFFERTY
MRS. DELLA M. CLUNN	MRS. ESTELLE J. SCHWERTLY
LAURA S. BUGBEE	HAZEL L. HAGERMAN
Sewing	Music
A. LAURA KELLY	ANNE LAFFERTY
Drawing and Manual Training	Physical Training

D. W. DAVIS
Supervising Principal

BOARD OF EDUCATION

GEORGE L. SWYLER
President

MRS. ELIZABETH K. BOSTWICK	FRANK W. MEVES
District Clerk	Chairman Property Committee
Chairman Teachers' Committee	
DAYTON R. LUDWIG	WALTER S. SLACK
Chairman Supply Committee	Chairman Finannce Committee

**The Eighth-Grade Graduation
of Pitman Public Schools.** The
Class of 1925 motto was "The door
to success is labeled Push."

READY FOR THE FOURTH OF JULY PARADE, C. 1948. From left to right are ? Montgomery, Gar Shaw, Bobbie Blakeslee, Rich Mangano, Ronny Blakeslee, Judy Scott, Jerry Blakeslee, Sam Downs, and John Roos.

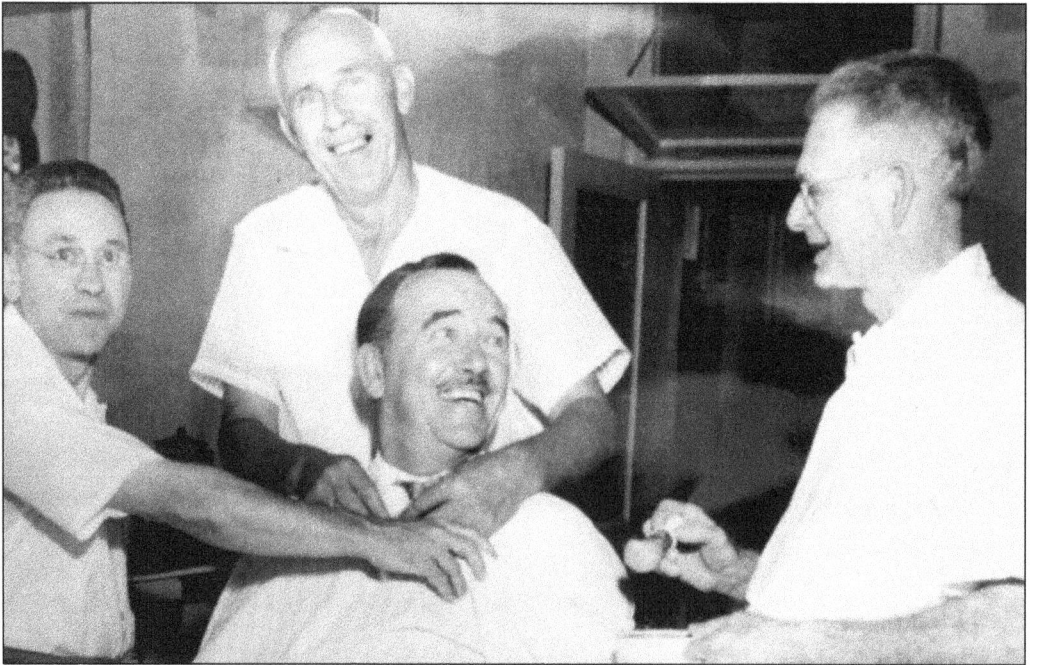

ACTOR PRESTON FOSTER'S VISIT DURING PITMAN'S 50TH ANNIVERSARY, 1955. Preston Foster (seated, center) gets the works. With him, from left to right, are barber Joe Mangano, Paul Carew, and barber George Kirshner.

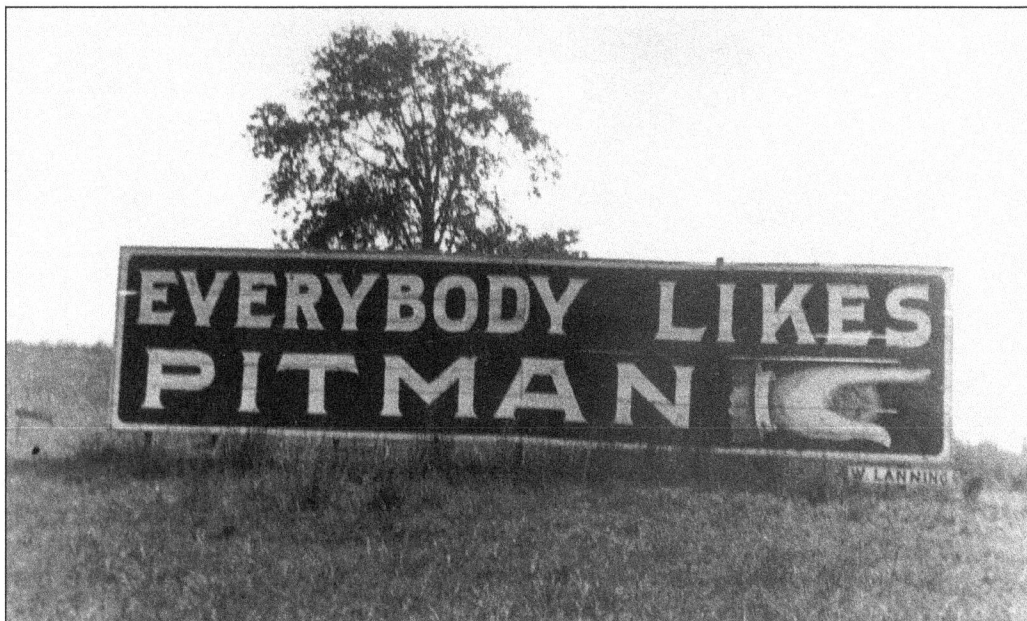

"Everybody Likes Pitman," the Slogan of Mary Dilks, 1913. The winner of Pitman's 1913 slogan contest was chosen from more than 300 entries. The slogan is still used today.

The Itaska Indian Fountain in Ballard Park, c. 1950. This monument was vandalized many times by high school rivals of Pitman and lost its head in the early 1960s. The Indian disappeared a few years later. The fountain was also removed. West Jersey Avenue is in the background.

PITMAN'S WINDMILL. This windmill was built on the Walter H. Moore estate in 1929. It is located on Grant Avenue. The four vanes of the windmill are 44 feet high. The top windows offer a majestic view of Pitman.

A CITRATE OF MAGNESIA BOTTLE, C. THE 1930S. This bottle was from the Webb & Lodge drugstore. Remember, "Keep Well Corked."

THREE FAMILIAR BADGES OF THEIR DAY. From left to right are a Pitman Cottagers' Association badge from 1915, a Pitman Fire Patrol badge from 1905, and a Lizzie Smith Temple badge from 1920.

THREE UNDATED BADGES FROM PITMAN. Organized in 1901, Pitman Fire Company No. 1 is still serving Pitman today. G.R. Wood's bus company was started in July 1924 and ran for many years. "Marshal, Pitman, NJ" is thought to be a very early police badge.

LICENSE PLATE TOPPERS, THE 1950S. These are rare pieces today but were once a common decoration to any car license plate.

A BRASS PLAQUE, C. 1900. This brass plaque reads, "Alcyon Park." It served as the top piece to a National cash register and was probably at the entrance to the park. Note the fancy scrollwork on either side.

A RIBBON FROM PITMAN'S 50TH ANNIVERSARY, C. 1955. Although Pitman Grove was established in 1871, the town of Pitman was not incorporated until 1905. Note Robert Crowther's logo for Pitman's Golden Jubilee.

THREE PITMAN SCHOOL TRACK RIBBONS, 1926, 1927, AND 1931. May Day track meets were big events in the 1920s and 1930s.

AN EARLY PITMAN BOARD OF TRADE STICKER, C. 1920. The Pitman Board of Trade did much to promote the town. In 1906, the board published a pamphlet entitled *The Story of Pitman: A Plea for Rural Life*, written by William McFarland. It urged readers to "escape the many evils which of necessity must be endured in large cities."

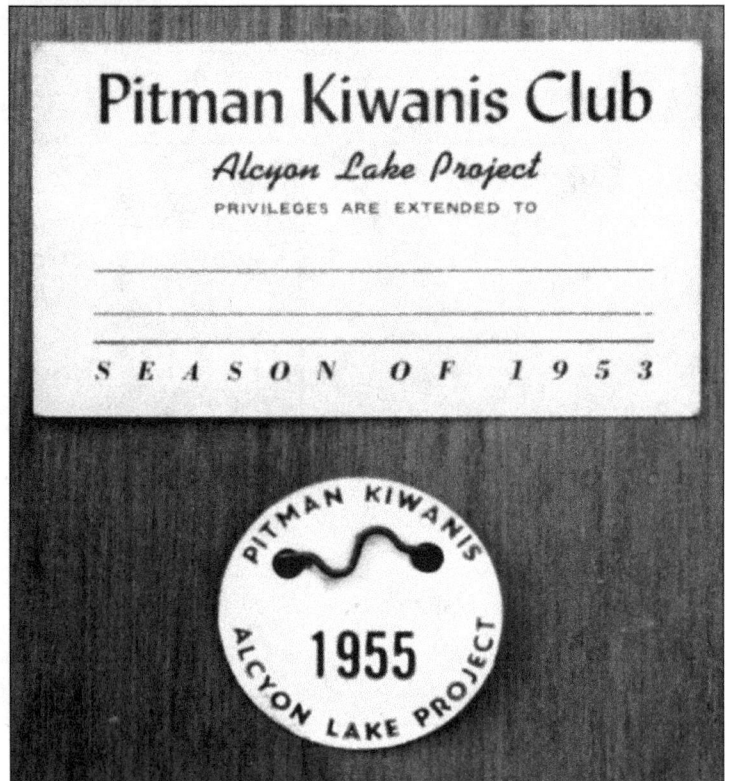

AN ALCYON LAKE PASS, 1953, AND AN ALCYON LAKE BADGE, 1955. Starting in 1951, the Pitman Kiwanis Club maintained the lake for residents and their guests.

A SEVENTH AVENUE HOUSE, PITMAN GROVE, C. 1900. This was a bed and breakfast of its day. It advertised private sleeping quarters for ladies and gentlemen, by the day or week. It was owned by G.W. Elkins and T.F. Tomlin.

A BADGE FOR THE DEDICATION OF NEW STREETS, OCTOBER 28, 1922. In the early 1920s, the town of Pitman, with county and state aid, undertook its first major paving program. This program was at a cost of more than $70,000, and the gravel road was on its way out.

A Movie Poster from Hunt's Park Theatre. This movie poster is from the 1922 silent film *Burning Sands*. The movie played at the Hunt's Park Theatre, which was located at the southeast corner of Pitman Avenue and West Jersey Avenue. It starred notables such as Wanda Hawley, Milton Sills, and Robert Cain.

A Movie Poster from the Broadway Theatre, c. 1949. Note the stars of a bygone era, such as Greer Garson in *That Forsyte Woman*, Tyrone Power in *The Prince of Foxes*, and Errol Flynn, Walter Pidgeon, and Robert Young. Last but certainly not least is Pitman's own Preston Foster in the 1939 movie *Geronimo*.

A COLLAGE OF PITMAN MEMORABILIA. The upper left section of this collage shows an advertising pass for Alcyon Track, an official race program, a Lucky Teter "Will See You at the Fair" pin, a Pitman Fire Patrol pin, and a Lizzie Smith Temple pin. The upper right section shows a Pitman Hotel advertising thermometer (1955), an Alcyon Track pass, an Alcyon Speedway ticket, a "Brothers of the Bush" Golden Jubilee pin, a May Day track meet ribbon (1926), and a Seventh Avenue restaurant business card. The lower right section features a Pitman Cottagers' Association pin (1915), a new streets dedication pin (1922), a marshal's badge, and a Kiwanis Club lake pass (1953). The lower left section has a 50th-anniversary ribbon (1955), a piece of Pitman Fire Company memorabilia, an Alcyon Lake theater ticket, a Harry Rulon Meat Market pencil holder, and an Alcyon Speedway souvenir pin.

O.B. CHEW ICE CREAM PARLORS, 1906. The ice-cream parlor was located at the corner of Broadway and Holly Avenue. The parlor used only Crane's pure ice cream. This ink blotter was given out to regular customers to promote the business.

Sen. John Hunt, c. 1968. Pitmanite John Hunt served as a state senator from 1963 to 1966. He served in the U.S. House of Representatives from 1967 to 1974.

The Logo for the Pitman Golden Jubilee Celebration, 1955. Pitman had its Golden Jubilee in 1955. This logo was designed by Robert W. Crowther and was a very popular image. It is still used today.

A National Trotting Association Certificate, 1935. This certificate shows that Alcyon Track and Sports Inc. paid the annual fee for membership in 1935. Harness racing was popular at the Alcyon Track, especially during the Gloucester County Grange Fair.

A New Jersey State Athletic Commission License, 1937. Some of the sporting events held at Alcyon Track did not include horses, cars, or baseball. A ring would be set up in front of the main grandstand, and boxing, sparring, or wrestling matches would be held.

The
Pitman Cook Book

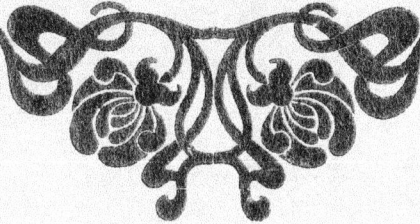

Compiled By

The Church Aid Society

Of The

Methodist Episcopal Church
Pitman, New Jersey

1909

THE PITMAN COOKBOOK, 1909. This cookbook was printed by Review Printing of Pitman. The cookbook was compiled by the Church Aid Society of the Methodist Episcopal Church in Pitman. Women sent in recipes, and local businessmen assisted by their advertisements to raise money for the church.

THE TABLET COMMEMORATING THE PITMAN MEN IN WORLD WAR I. In August 1919, W.C.K. Walls was appointed chairman of a citizens committee to place a tablet on a granite boulder commemorating the Pitman men who served in World War I. In 1952, it was moved to make it a part of the War Memorial Mall. Elwood Kindle was Pitman's lone casualty of the war.